This Crazy Cats Coloring Book

Belongs To:

....

Copyright ©
All rights reserved. No part of this publication may be reproduced, distributed,
or transmitted in any form or by any means, including photocopying, recording,
or other electronic or mechanical methods, without the prior written permission
of the publisher, except in the case of brief quotations embodied in critical reviews
and certain other noncommercial uses permitted by copyright law.

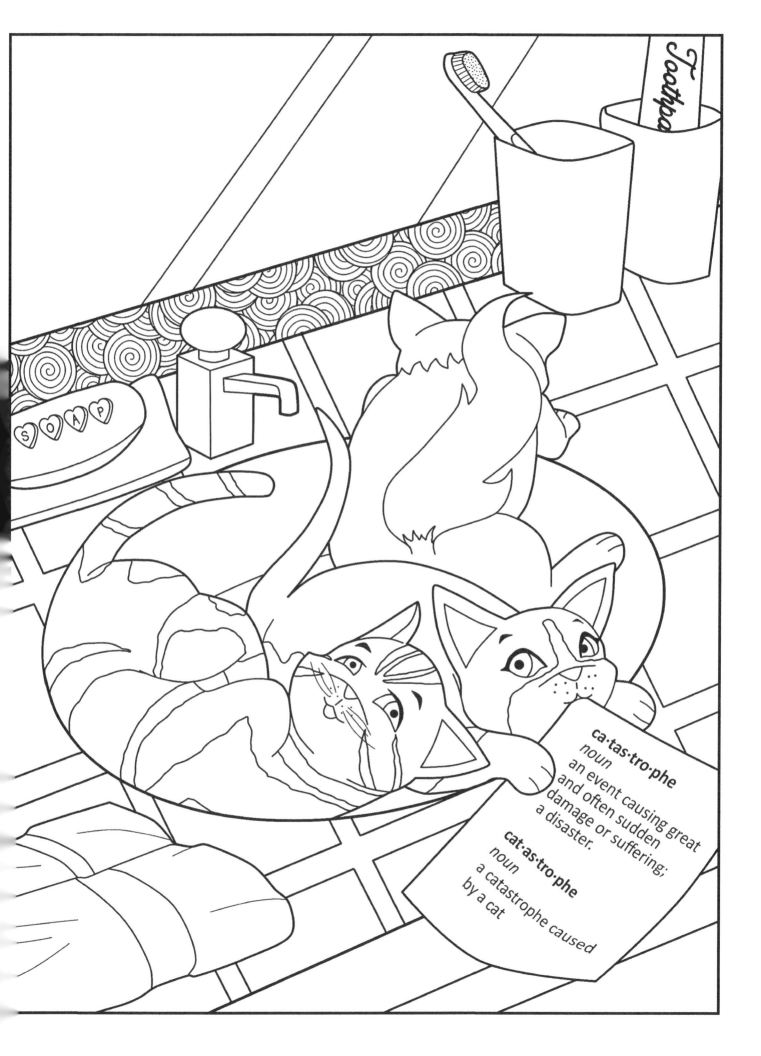

There will be CONSEQUENCES

Human. My bowl is empty.

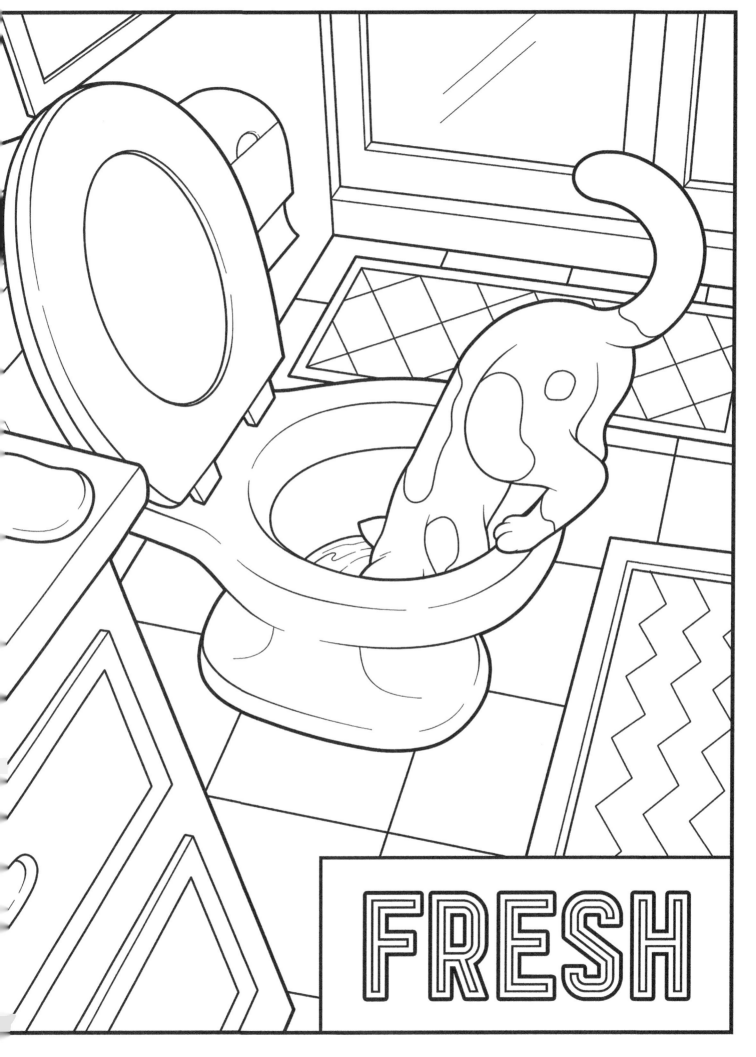

What? You've never had a bad ear day?

It tastes better when it's fresh.

Made in the USA
Monee, IL
25 July 2022